Brainstorming

Brainstorming

✦

Techniques for New Ideas

Timothy Cory with Thomas Slater

iUniverse, Inc.
New York Lincoln Shanghai

Brainstorming
Techniques for New Ideas

iUniverse, Inc.

For information address:
iUniverse, Inc.
2021 Pine Lake Road, Suite 100
Lincoln, NE 68512
www.iuniverse.com

ISBN: 0-595-29831-1 (pbk)
ISBN: 0-595-75140-7 (cloth)

Printed in the United States of America

Welcome to a New World of Ideas & Thinking.

What is *Brainstorming*? *Brainstorming* is a process of freethinking, not being bound by restraints such as: is the idea good or bad? Does it work? Will it sell?

Brainstorming is meant to produce an abundance of ideas. Some may be good, some bad, and others might be brilliant. Most importantly, let your ideas flow. At this point, there is no such thing as a bad idea. So, have some fun.

Where do we find creative ideas? We find them in The Maybe, The Possible, The What If, The Who Knows, and The Unknown. Truth is, you can find an idea just about anywhere. It's all about knowing where to begin. The ten techniques in this book will give you new ways in which to stimulate your creative process. Each technique will show you a process to open up another part of your subconscious to allow the ideas to flow free.

This book is dedicated to my family—my wife Jan, my two children Romi and Rocki (the dogs) who have been so supportive of me throughout my career by allowing me time and opportunity to pursue my dreams. For all of the times I was out of town for the birthdays, anniversaries or coming home late, I thank you.

Goldfish and Rainbows! TIM

To my partner and best friend, Tom—Thanks for the friendship and all the fun we've had creating some great advertising while always looking at what's truly important "LUNCH."

TIM

Contents

Introduction

Float like a butterfly, sting like a bee.

—Muhammad Ali

Today's businesses need to think faster on their feet than ever before. They have to change and adapt almost daily to keep up with their customers' appetites for better products and services, constantly searching for that next business building idea, that marketing insight that will take them to the top.

Unfortunately, unlike the businesses, many advertising agencies haven't been so eager or quick to respond to today's ever changing business demands. While the retailer (advertiser) has more need than ever to focus his energy up front on the tough stuff—coming up with new business building ideas and insight—the ad agency seems content to deliver on the easy part: the ads. Why should this change? Change is unsettling. It's risky. And after all, risk is the other business destiny.

Fact is you can't change an agency that doesn't understand or isn't equipped to do the job. Many ad people haven't been trained as marketers. They've been trained in an antiquated industry to be executors instead of admen. A true adman is someone who solves marketing problems, and who is turned on by moving merchandise, and who knows that ads are merely one of the tools and skills needed to build a client's business. What's really important is the idea!

Whether agencies accept it or not, the advertising business is moving more toward the thinkers and doers and away from the executors and order takers. Why? Because anybody can execute a commercial. And anybody can carry a bag to get a client approval. Why should a client pay for these services when they don't significantly impact their business? They should only pay for something that adds value to their business. Ideas that generate new business and increase profits are worth paying for and paying well.

Dare we suggest there is some better way out there for the retailer (advertiser)? Something that can fill the cavernous gap between lazy thinking and ad executions?

> *Far better it is to dare mighty things than to live in the gray twilight that knows not victory nor defeat.*

—Theodore Roosevelt

Dare Mighty Thing thinkers and doers are people who have a passion for digging into a business with an uncanny instinct for the big idea. A group of people who move fast to concentrate and focus on what really matters—the work up front, that business building idea, that unique insight that can take a client's business over the top.

Advertising isn't for the faint of heart.
It takes imagination, wisdom, and a healthy dose of guts.
It takes the courage to Dare Mighty Things.

This book is a compilation of our more than twenty-five plus years of advertising experience, as well as mentoring from other great creative minds. It's devoted to new ideas and new techniques in generating ideas. Techniques that will aid you in "expanding your universe of thought," not just get you to "think outside the box." The techniques in the following chapters are designed so that they help to open your subconscious imagination to possibilities that your conscious would rule out. What we want you to get is that every one is creative everyday, people just need to have doors opened for them. All of these techniques to follow are doors to your creativity.

Over our many years, we have seen students come out of school without really knowing how to get from point "A" to point "B". Now, we're not saying that they're not talented because so many of them are, and they have wonderful portfolios; but, creative without strategy can be good to look at and to read, but it doesn't serve the client. A 'good creative' needs to look at the entire picture:

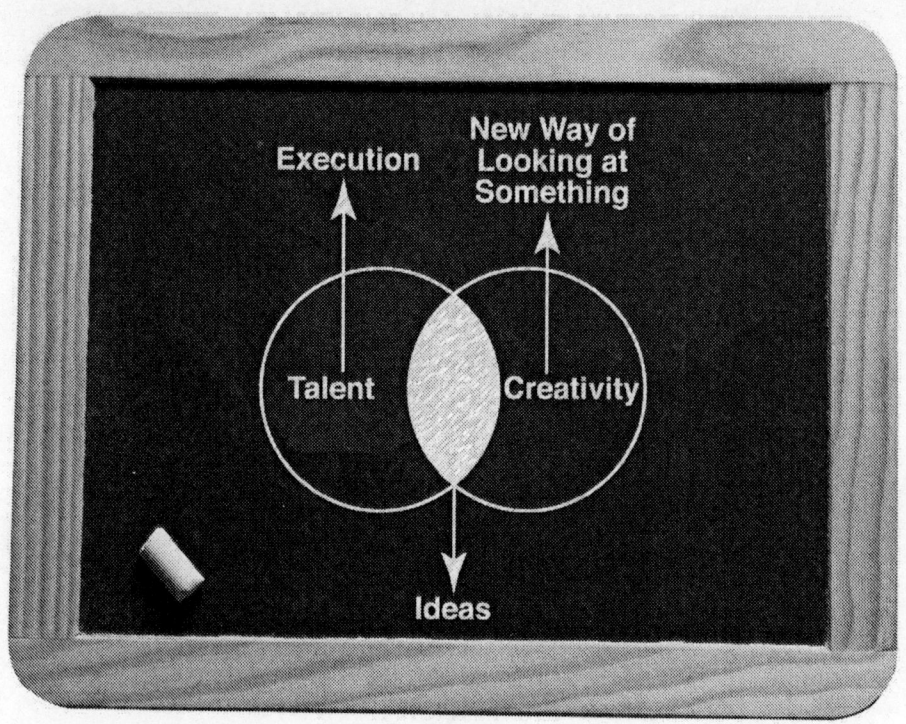

Good Concept + Good Strategy = Selling Product and Increasing Profit.

Remember, the way we all keep our jobs is by increasing our clients' profits (and good creative ideas can do that).

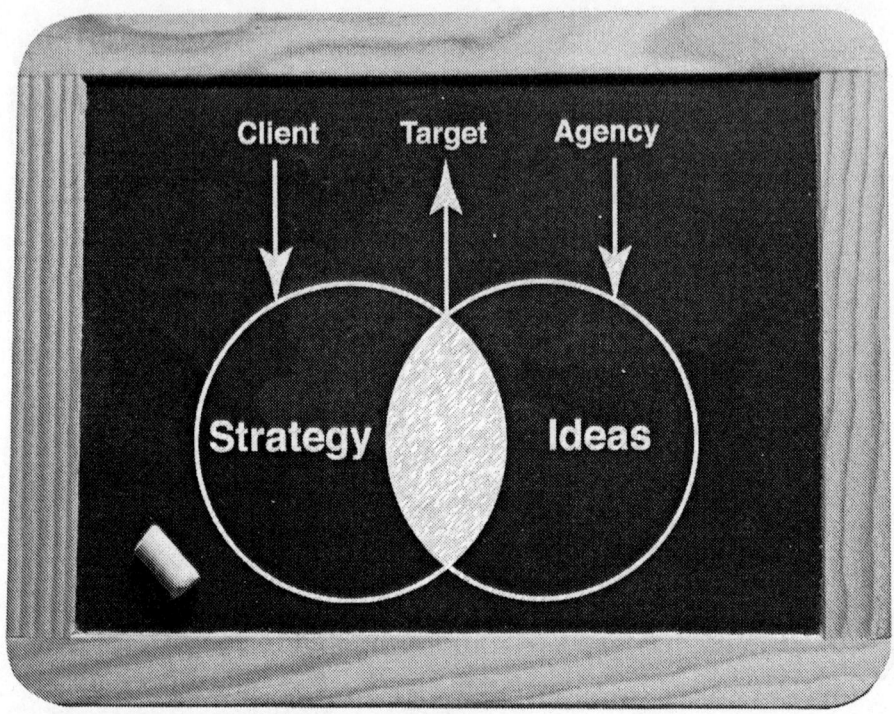

Discovering the difference between work that is well executed on a thin and shallow base—and work that is deep and resonant with strong, big, brand building ideas. [1]

In the chapters to follow, we will discuss *Brainstorming* techniques. Techniques that can be applied to more than just advertising but to any business or invention creating process. They can be used to solve all types of problems or used to create new products never before seen. We will walk through the process of creating an idea, from how to start, to different ways in which to generate ideas. We will also learn to identify Creative Strategy and make that strategy work for you in creating ideas that work for your client.

---

1.   Quote by: Andrew Jaffe, Executive Director, Clio Awards, Publishing Director of Adweek Books

1

What is Creativity?

huh?

Before we dive into actual brainstorming techniques, let's focus briefly on Creativity and Left vs. Right Brain Thinking. What is creativity? It is the *inspiration* of looking at something in a new or unique way. The definition of *creativity* is: inventive, to cause to come into existence; make; originate, to bring about; give rise to, to stimulate the inventive powers. The word "inspiration" is based on a Greek word meaning the God within; to motivate by divine influence, to create. Everybody is creative! We are all capable of problem solving and problem solving is creativity. Even though most people consider themselves just moderately creative, solving more day-to-day problems, a small portion of the population has true creativity—the ability to bring about change in people and the world around them.

Children are creative explosions. It can be said that kids are 100% creative. It's not until they learn to be judgmental of their ideas that they loose that ability and become more adult in their thinking. Then they drop to more or less 30% creative. Kids are inventive and open to the impossible. They are dreamers with little limitations to their imagination. Those of us who keep that kid inside will always be creative with the ability to change people's perceptions of the world. Keep an open mind to the unusual and let your imagination wander—and daydream once in awhile. Daydreaming is healthy for the mind...and the soul.

Left Brain vs. Right Brain Thinkers. There's always much discussion about which side of the brain is more dominant in a person. Left brain thinkers are supposed to be more analytical and right brain thinkers more creative.

Left Brain is the "right-handed," left-hemisphere mode. The Left is foursquare, upright, sensible, direct, true, hard-edged, un-fanciful, forceful, analytical, and predictable.

Right Brain is the "left-handed," right-hemisphere mode. The Right is curvy, flexible, more playful in its unexpected twists and turns, more complex, diagonal, fanciful, emotional, and visual.

Does this mean that all left-handed people are more creative? NO! Does it mean that right-handed people are less? NO! It means that we all use different processes to solve problems creatively. With this said, some basic generalizations can be made as to how each side of the brain works and what its duties are:

Creativity and Left vs. Right Brain Thinking.

Left Brain Thinkers	Right Brain Thinkers
step-by-step reasoning	mystical
logical	musical
mathematical	"creative"
speaking	visual-pictorial
dominates right brain	submissive to the left brain
pattern user	pattern seeker

Whether you are left-handed or right-handed, it makes no difference to your level of creativity. All it shows is the process by which you might reach your goals.

2

Creative Strategy

✦

*the why? what? where?
when? and who?*

Where to start? Let's begin by asking ourselves a few questions that will help us to determine our objective. Without an objective we can go nowhere. Always remember, the more you know, the more you can problem solve. So let's begin: Why are we doing what we are asked to do? Who is the consumer? Why do they want our product or service? What can we say? What makes us different from our competitors? What advantages do we have? What is our final goal? Strategy is about why, what, where, when, who? You must understand a client's business to find out what it is that will make them different from their competitors. To go from point "A" (strategy) to point "B" (idea) you must have a plan.

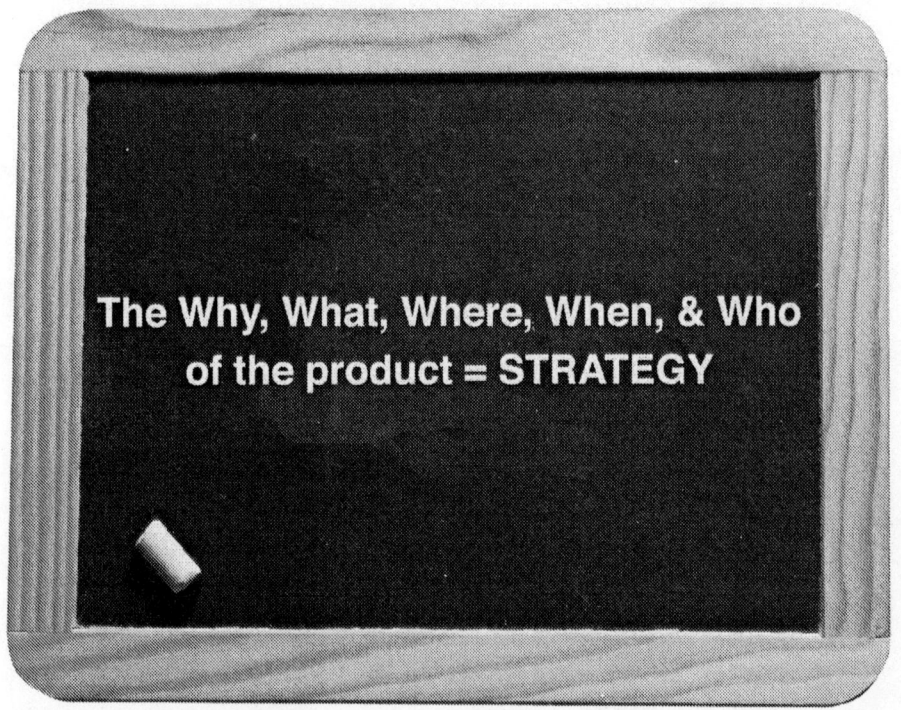

Once you've asked all the questions based on the client, ask them again, based on the audience (consumer).

Why are we doing what we are doing? Huh? There needs to be a reason for what we are doing if we intend to be successful at it. Do we want people to eat more hamburgers? Do we want customers to rush into a 24-hour sale? Do we want to create a certain image/brand for a company? Do we want to build upon a product's prestige?

What makes our product so special? If it's a vitamin, it helps keep people healthy. It may be easy to swallow or taste really great. What stores sell it? When asking 'what' get inside and outside the product. Learn all that you can. Know all that you can know. In order to sell a product we need to know that product. Even small things can later become big ideas if we ask lots of questions and write down all the answers.

If it's a package good your advertising, write down all of the ingredients as-well-as the nutritional information. If it's a car, write down all of the features and special options available as-well-as how much horsepower, torque, or cargo room is available.

Where is the product used? In a kitchen, bath, at work? Where helps define not only the product for you but also the consumer you are trying to convince.

Also ask where the idea is to be showcased. While the consumer is sitting, standing, lying? Are they in their house, at work, at play? You may ask, what does this matter? Clarifying all of this information in your mind will help you to create a better idea…that works and reaches your audience!

When is much like *where* but addresses time. When is the product to be used? At mealtime, before bed, in the morning, when something is broken?

Also ask when will the idea be seen? When is the best time to present them with the idea? AM or PM? Before they eat or after? At work or at home?

Finally, ***Who*** are we talking to? Consider age, gender and economic situation of the consumer. Can the young use it as well as the old? Is it just for a certain age group? Will women want it more than men or is it just made for one sex to use? Can people afford our product? Who can afford it? Who is the product targeted towards? Who wants it? Who really cares?

Think of every project as a journey, make it so specific to its time and place that it becomes completely new, allowing you to invent in a fresh environment that's full of energy.[1]

Once you've spent some time answering these basic questions and writing them down. Prioritize the most important questions and answers. Use these as your *roadmap* or *creative strategy* to follow as we move forward with generating new ideas.

NOTE: It's always helpful to put things on a blackboard or on a wall. This way you can see the full picture or strategy at one glance. Get used to doing this—you won't regret it!

Example: Our client, Sanford Confections, wants to re-introduce the protein-packed, 'good for you' candy bar, Grady's Glorious Bar, Grady's has long been considered a 'kids' candy bar, but client wants to expand the market to include active adults.

Grady's Glorious Candy Bar

Why?	—to sell more candy bars.
	—to re-introduce the product to the public
	—to target adults as well as kids
What?	—chocolate and oat protein packed candy bar
	—'good for you' candy bar
	—known as a kids' candy bar
Where?	—print/magazines/sports oriented
	—at: the gym, home, park, drive to work, playing with the kids
When?	—while exercising, playing, working,
	—tired…when you need a 'pick me up'
	—when you need a sweet but want something healthy

---

1.   Murry Gelberg, Graphic Design, May 2002 page 35

Who?   —active adults

                        —kids

                        —people on the go

                        —the health conscious

The above is a simplified strategy but hopefully you get the idea.

When we talk about creative strategy, we must also consider Image vs. Need. Do I want the product because I believe it will make me better or do I need the product to help me survive, do something better than before, or plain help me to do something?

Image is just that—to change someone's perception of the product and how they imagine it in their life.

Need is both I have to have it to survive as well as I need it to do something easier or better than with out it.

Consider that Image vs. Need will have a great impact on how you are going to market the product or service. And remember—*image* may be the reason someone *needs* a product. It can be so confusing.

Where do ideas come from? We find them in The Maybe, The Possible, The What If, The Who Knows, and The Unknown. Truth is, you can find an idea just about everywhere. The use of knowledge interaction combined with imagination is how ideas take form. From an acorn to an oak tree there is a process of growth. The better the soil and the elements the bigger and faster the oak tree (IDEA) will grow.

> *All our knowledge has its origin in our perceptions*
>
> —Leonardo Da Vinci[2]

Pareto: namely, that an idea is nothing more nor less than a new combination of old elements. Idea is a new combination, and the ability to make new combinations is heightened by an ability to see relationships within things.[3]

---

2.   How to think like Leonardo Da Vinci. By Michael J. Gelb, Page 95

3.   A Technique for Producing Ideas by James Webb Young, page 25

You can only generate ideas based on what you know, have seen, or have experienced. To be a good generator of ideas you must first have many life experiences. There is nothing new…ideas are the make-up of a shake and bake of your experiences and knowledge. New Inventions or Ideas are just a new way of looking at something that you already know and creating a new way based on your experience to do something differently. Therefore, to be a great idea generator, you must diversify your knowledge. For example; read about different subjects, travel to different parts of the world, play different kinds of music, and do different sports/activities. Experience life and you will enjoy life both at work and home. At a point in your life in advertising you will notice that generating ideas is a twenty-four hour occupation and you'll love it.

A lifetime of experience and stimulation funnels down into that one perfect nugget.[4]

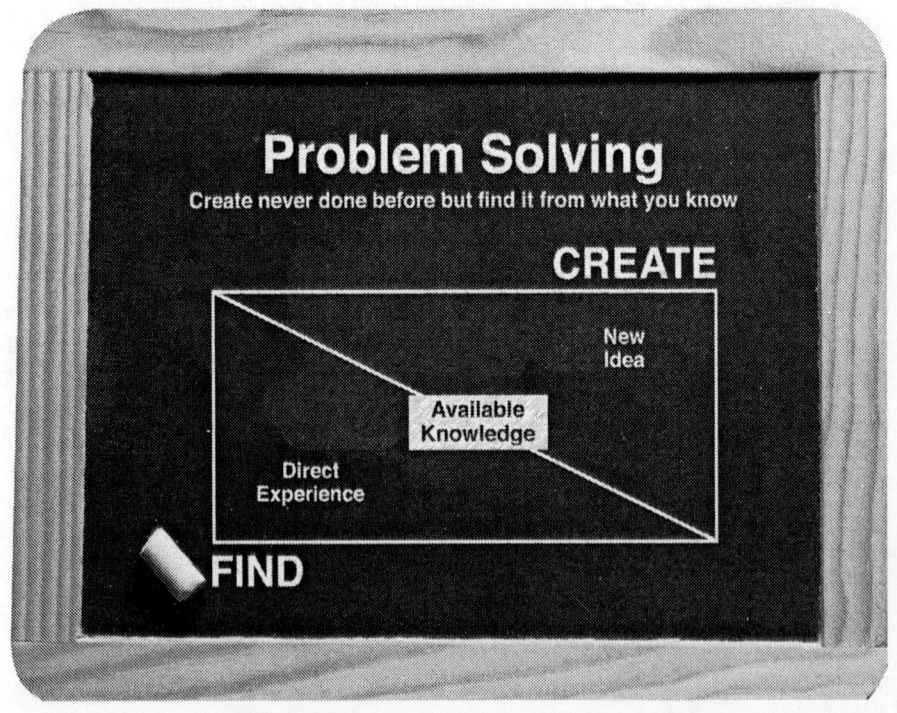

---

4.   How Do You Get Ideas? By Robyn Griggs in the publication "AGENCY" Fall 1996 page 36

Ideas are always there; we just have to find them. It's more detective work than divine inspiration. There's always oil, but sometimes it's at the bottom of the North Sea.[5]

Everything you can imagine is real

—Pablo Picasso

Creativity = Problem Solving = Selling.[6] How can we create ideas when we stare at a blank sheet of paper? The following are ten ways in which we can help ourselves to think about problem solving. These are not the only ways, but for our purpose, we will use these ten.

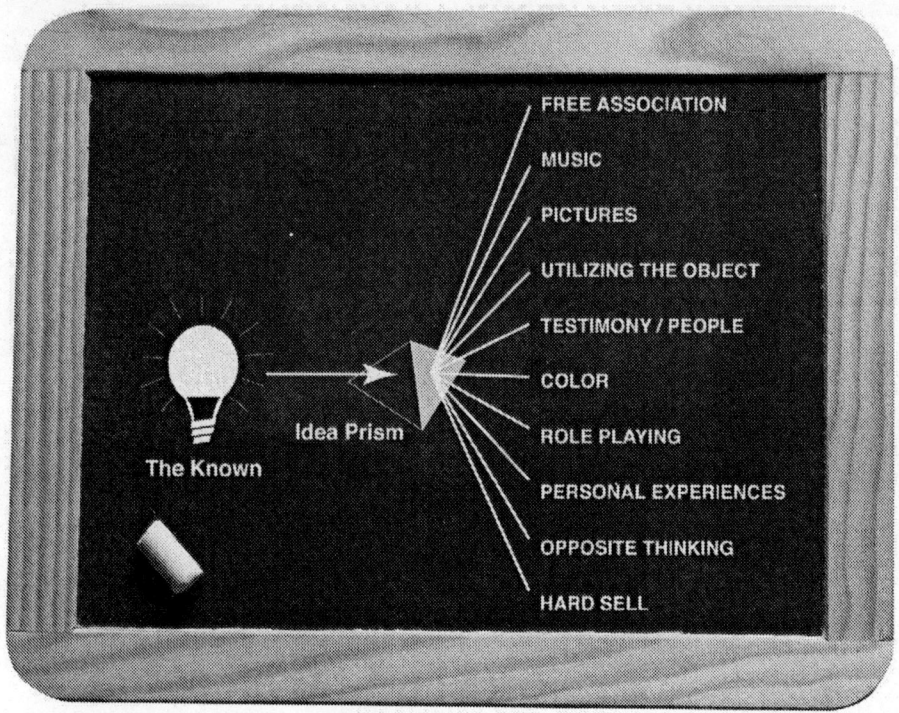

By using what you know and using one of the ten techniques we will cover in the following chapters, ideas will start to take shape.

---

5. Jim Bosha, Executive VP Executive Creative Director, Campbell Mithun Esty, Minneapolis—Quote
6. Tom Monaham "Creativety" Seminar 1997

Notes

3

Free Association

◆

letting it all go

Free Association is about not thinking structurally, but thinking by relaxing your mind and letting it all come out. It's not about judging good or bad, right or wrong, will it work or not? It's about opening up your subconscious to all possibilities—letters, numbers, names, places, stories, objects and even just doodles. One of the most difficult things for us to do is to just let go and not try to justify why we are writing something down or thinking a certain way. If you feel it, put it down. It doesn't have to be on a line or even an even plane. It may be in a circle, upside down, whatever. Let yourself go! We cannot stress this enough for this technique to work. Some of the best ideas come from the strangest of places. If you never get to those places, you won't ever discover the idea.

> *Out of nowhere the Idea will appear. It will come to you when you least expect it.*
>
> —James Webb Young, A Technique for Producing Ideas[1]

By not censoring your thoughts through free association, you can relax your mind and allow yourself to think about the strategy and the product without operating on a pre-determined course. Many times when we are relaxed and not trying to think about something that is when our thinking is the clearest and most precise.

Exercise One: Structuring your line of consciousness. Pick a product. Develop your creative strategy (*Why? What? Where? When? and Who?*).

Re-read it. Now, open your mind and just write. Write everything that enters your mind down. Don't stop for at least ten minutes. Just keep on writing. Ideas...the time you need to pick up the dry cleaning...What's for dinner? Absolutely everything! Don't worry about grammar, spelling or sentence structure. This is about opening your mind to all possibilities. Thinking about not being able to think is, in fact, thinking. Write that down.

Now go back to your product and creative strategy. Does anything from your 'freethinking' stand out? Does it help you look at the product in a different way? How can you make it work, can you see the beginnings of an idea that relates back to the product? Through all of the words, thoughts, phrases, and doodles

---

1.   A Technique for Producing Ideas by James Webb Young, Page 4

your mind should start to make some connections or other thoughts (ideas) may pop into your head.

Exercise Two: Line of consciousness. Pick a product. Develop your creative strategy. Now, ask a hundred questions about the product. Do not stop to answer them. After a hundred questions (you can also set a time limit), pick the ten best and then ask ten questions about each of those questions. Pick the two best of those and answer them by continually writing everything about the two questions that you can. Return to your product and strategy. Does anything work? You should be able to make it work you have a lot to choose from by now.

Exercise Three: Another twist on free association. Pick a product and develop your creative strategy. Now, randomly select at least five words from the following list (or open up a dictionary or book and randomly select five nouns, adjectives or adverbs or look around you and make an impromptu list of the things you see).

AUTOMOBLIE	HORSE	COFFEE
RACING	OBESE	CAN
RIGID	WOOKBOOK	DANGEROUS
CHEF	ALLIGATOR	FROZEN
LEAN	DROWSY	SUPPLE
COLOR	FOLDER	KOSHER
FOOT	BLOSSOM	WALLET
BROTHER	HOPPING	ARGUMENT
POSTER	FOOTBALL	HUNGRY
COCKTAIL	MAGICIAN	PICTURE
HOSTAGE	BALLOON	COASTAL
MASSAGE	ROUGH	SUPERSTAR
REFRIGERATOR	PLANT	OVERLOAD
SAFETY NET	CEILING	BOOKCASE
SWEET	HOST	ENVIRONMENT
LION	SOILED	EXPEDITION

RECORD	PENCIL	PRETTY
MONEY	CRIMINAL	TELEPHONE
PUDDING	PHOTO	KISS
JERSEY	CONVENIENCE	SENSOR
POWERFUL	RUGGED	ULTIMATE
INCLUSIVE	LAKESIDE	INTERIOR
SOFTNESS	EXCLUSIVE	REQUIREMENT
BELT	EGGSHELL	REFLECTIVE
FULL-SIZE	ELECTRONIC	SLIPPERY
UNEVEN	WISHBONE	FOOLISH

Now take each selected word and come up with three ideas relating to the product for each. Can you do it? Yes, you can! You may ask, "how does this help me?" By writing down everything we are thinking we are allowing our mind to process a ton of information and access areas of the mind we may not normally use to solve a problem or answer a question. Remember, we are looking for a place to begin, some place that stimulates other thoughts that connects back to the product.

Expanding the Universe. Now that you have an idea there is always a need to look further with each thought starter you have. The universe in which that thought lives is much bigger if we but look a little further. It has the possibility to never end. We can do this by mapping out thoughts or ideas. The diagram below is a spiral universe or the rings of growth of a tree, always expanding outward. The thought (word) needs to be expanded and to grow if we hope for the idea to go from good to great. Much like a city or tree grows, so will your thoughts and ideas.

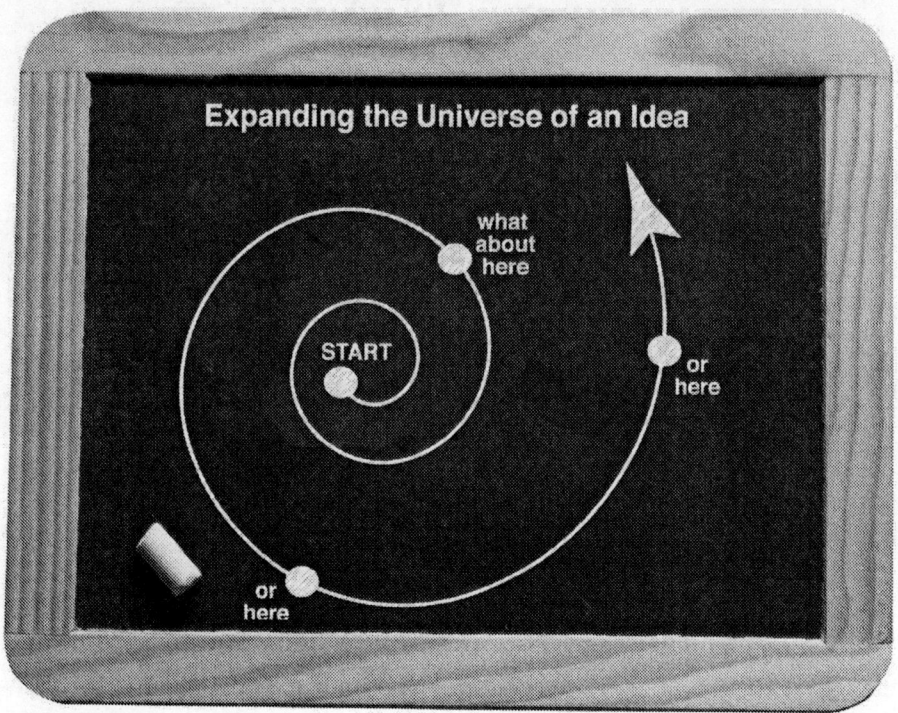

Mapping as shown in the next diagram illustrates how an idea can be expanded out much like a tree's branches and roots. The idea is the world you live in at that moment. By starting with a single idea and expanding it with words that you can associate with that idea, you are expanding that idea's universe and opening up the possibilities for a great idea to be found.

An example of this: In your free association you choose the word green as your thought starter. From green we could write the word *grass,* then long, short, wet, rye, blue, Kentucky, brown, barley, wheat, hard, soft, and brittle. From each of these words we could expand to new branches and roots.

Green could also take us to meanings such as life. *Life* could then be expanded to words like new, born, baby, small, little, energy, renew, rejuvenate, beginning, start, and so on. You get the idea. It can be endless and all of these words may generate a new idea for the product or a new direction for us to follow. Once again, remember—you're looking for a place to begin. The mind will eventually make connections and generate many ideas.

Once you have all of these words to work with, look back to the creative strategy. Which words might fit into the strategy? Is there a word that helps to explain or describe to someone what it is you are selling? It's all about creating an image, a story, or an emotion in the consumer's mind that will help create a desire and decision to buy your idea and the product.

Notes

4

Music

✦

many styles for many ideas

Music is something we all can relate to. It reminds us of our experiences: love, friendship, youth, location, home, feelings, or time. Because of this, listening to music is an ideal way to generate ideas. The different music styles can be used to generate all kinds of different ideas. Music can also be very visual. These visuals may be represented as—flashy, quick cuts, long dissolves, funky, or layered. It can represent visually all the emotions that have happened to us.

Trust what you feel.[1]

To generate different ideas purchase five different types of music to listen to while thinking of ideas. Lets start with Jazz and think of the client's product and imagine it with that beat. What comes to your mind? Let it go. Feel the music. The more you imagine the notes dancing to the beat the more your mind can open up to all the possibilities. The list of music styles to follow is not complete, but it should get you to think of all the different types of music that are available to listen to and enjoy.

Jazz: At its best, jazz is a dance between chaos and order, filled with expression and inspiration in the essence of creativity. You'll discover that as you listen to some of the greatest jazz musicians like Louis Armstrong, Duke Ellington, and Ella Fitzgerald that this all-American musical style is some of the most amazing and complicated music to listen to. Other newer bands might be the Yellow Jackets, Earl Klue, and Spiro Gyro.

These are just a few words you could use to describe jazz music: cool, fast, playful, smokey, quick, long, dark, joyous, dramatic, loud, horns, drums, guitar, wind, flute, piano, ivory, keys, sharp, flat, repetitive, water, floating, adrift, stormy, flowing, etc…

How about other thoughts and images that come to mind: 1940, festivals, The South, New Orleans, Mardi Gras, Bourbon Street, spicy food, swamps, Chicago, Montroux-Detroit, etc…Get the idea? By writing down all the words that come to mind when we listen to music we are able to visualize our feeling.

Next try classical. This will tell more of a story in its melody. See if you can hear cultural differences and the different historical styles. In classical music,

---

1.   Murry Gelberg, Ignition a publication by SAPPI Paper

Bach's highly structured, rule oriented music style communicates a respect for authority, both on the divine level and secular, that can be characterized by the Teutonic society in the Baroque period. Listen and try to let it all go again…see what happens. Try listening to Beethoven's 9th Symphony. You'll find it a treat to your ears, your mind and your soul. Listen to Vivaldi's *Four Seasons* or Mozart's violin concertos. Chopin is an influential and early Romantic composer. Discover how and why his music is as timeless as ever. This is by no means the end of the great classical music and composers available to you, but simply a starting point. Can you find an idea in the story, the structure of the notes, the types of instruments played, or the expression by which the timing of the notes are played? Music is about an emotional story that puts us into a time and place.

Rock: The musical rhythm of getting somewhere fast just because we should. Rock music is powerful, loud, rebellious, driving, challenging, and emotional. The short list of musical giants might be: Rolling Stones, Led Zeppelin, Journey, Wings, Kiss, the Beatles, and The Who. Rock music started in the 50's and continues to be popular in the 21st Century with many new bands putting out new work.

Blues: The ultimate in had, lost, wants, and beliefs. Blues is a complete expression of the musician and what they feel. They give all of their heart and soul to you through their music. Many of these musicians have suffered a lot to tell you their story in their words. It is because of these many crossroads that they have traveled in their careers that we are able to feel what they feel or have felt. A couple of great Blues musicians are Muddy Waters, B.B. King, and Steve Ray Vaughn. All have an unmistakable and recognizable style all their own.

Country: Much like the Blues, Country music is about had, lost, and wants with a little bit of twang put into it. Musicians like: Alan Jackson, Dolly Parton, and Clint Black. Some of the more Country/POP hybrids like Shania Twain, Faith Hill, Toby Keith, Tim McGraw to name just a few are also good choices. Country music is all about life and the hardships and joys associated with living it. If we look into the heart of country music we can find our countries pride and ourselves.

Ethnic: Can you here the country of origin in the music? Is the soul of the people there? Try listening to Latin music, Spanish, American Indian, Celtic, African, Japanese, Calypso, or Himalayan music. Music stores over the last ten years have acquired immense lists of music from other countries. Just because our product is made in America doesn't mean that an idea can't have a Latin, Oriental, or foreign feel to it.

As mentioned before, music can be a stimulant for many emotions like love, friendship, youth, place, home, feelings of sadness or happiness, or time itself. When you are listening to music while trying to generate ideas take great care in listening to your emotions as you listen to the music. Don't let this opportunity pass while you come to grips with your emotions. Make notes for yourself as to what you are feeling to certain pieces of music. This reference will help you at later times when trying to generate ideas for other products and clients.

Make sure that in your everyday life you expand your knowledge and listening habits to all types and styles of music that are out there.

Exercise: Go to the cupboard or closet and randomly choose an object. Then choose five different music styles to listen to while thinking of ideas. Maybe begin with jazz. Think of the product and imagine it with the beat. What comes to mind? Let it go. Feel the music. The more you imagine the notes dancing to the beat, the more your mind can open up to all the possibilities. Now list what the music means to you. How you feel? The things you remember. Next, look at the product. How does the music make you feel/think towards the product? Does it bring any situations to mind? Does it take place in a certain time period? What kind of person is playing or who is listening? What kind of visuals do you see? Where is the music being played? Do you see flashes, quick cuts, something funky? Remember to write down every word that comes to mind and everything you feel, this will be important as you move forward in the thinking process. This is not the time to be picky and there is no right or wrong. All of these words are important because what you feel about a piece of music, many times others will too. It's that insight which we are seeking.

Now try this with different music styles. Maybe classical, country, rock, blues, ethnic, or…

Once you have all your thoughts down on paper, look at the product and your notes. Does anything stand out? Connect the dots. Use the strategy of Why? What? Where? When? and Who? What ideas can you use to tell the product's story in an interesting way? All of the words you used to describe the music should now help in creating an idea for how to sell the product.

Notes

5

Pictures and Collages

✦

*a picture is worth
a thousand words*

Pictures and Collages. How do we go from picture to idea? The use of pictures, whether one or many, to present an idea is not a new concept. Cave painters from prehistoric times used pictorial images to convey ideas. We've all heard the saying that 'a picture is worth a thousand words' and this is very true. Pictures were some of the earliest forms of language. From cave drawings to Egyptian hieroglyphics to early medieval mosaics to the use of tavern signs to advertise food, lodging, or goods for sale, pictures have been an integral part of our visual language.

If we can see it, it must be true. That is human nature. This is why tabloids sell so many copies each week. If we see it, we want to believe that it's true. This is also the basis for much evidence used in a court of law. Some cases are won and lost on the belief of jurors without the help of an eyewitness. Because of this, a picture can be a very influential force in selling an idea.

Pictures like music can put the viewer into a time and a place. Pictures stimulate our senses…that's why burger joints and restaurants show you delicious, hot, mouth-watering images—it makes you hungry.

Ideas = show/give = telling a story.
Creativity = Problem Solving = Selling.

How are ideas found in a picture? Ideas will seem to come from images that have nothing to do with the client's product or service. They come because of the great many associations we have built up over the years through our life experiences. Remember—to be a good generator of ideas, you need to live life to its fullest so as to be able to make these associations.

Man can learn nothing unless he proceeds from the known to the unknown.
—Claude Bernard, French Physiologist

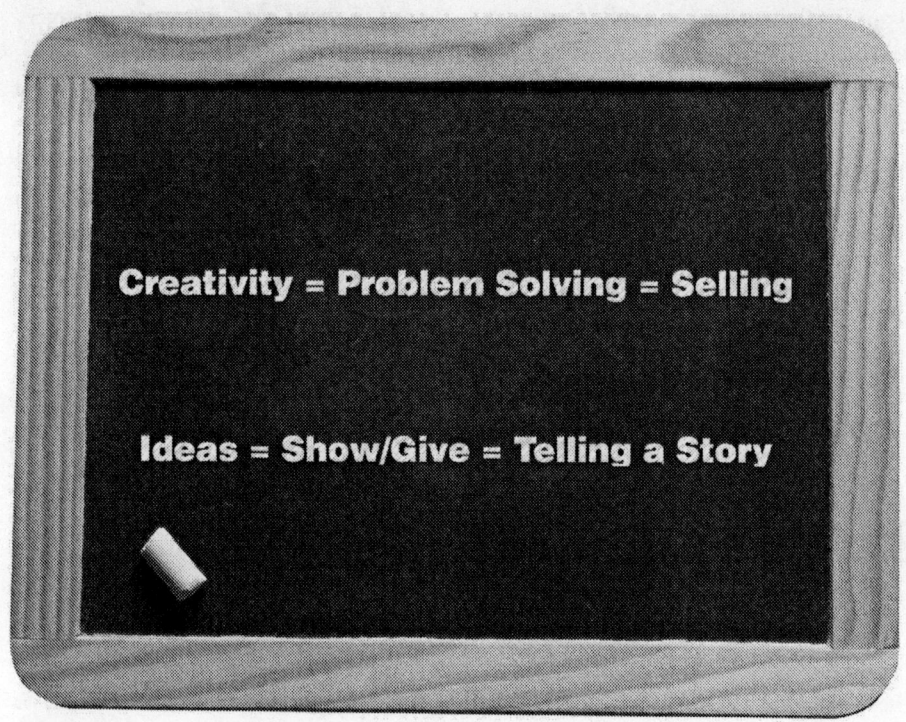

Exercise One: Working With Pictures. Remember to begin with the Why, What, Where, When, and Who of the product!

Let's begin our brainstorming with pictures by picking up a bunch of magazines that the client might advertise in or that the client's end user might read. Go through them and cut out other ads, pictures and articles. Cut out anything that strikes you or makes an impression. It doesn't have to relate to our product right now. Paste all of these pictures on a board or pin them up on a wall. Hopefully you are now starting to see a picture of who your user is. This should help you to start generating ideas of how everyone else is advertising this type of product. Don't just look at your competitors. See how everyone else is using pictures to advertise to the same demographics. We're not done yet!

Now go through some stock photography catalogs. There are also web-site available to you as well to find images (Stock Photo, Single Image, FPG, ibid, and Masterfile) Start by cutting photos of images that fit into your target market and add them to the wall. At the same time if you see something that catches your eye, cut it out as well. You don't have to have any reason for it at this very moment. We want our minds to open up to all the possibilities. Unconsciously, there might be an idea in that picture that your mind is trying to get out. We'll find it later. Once you have wall papered the room stand back and absorb the imagery for a while. As you observe all these images, look at how the client's product might fit into one of those images. Write on the photos the thoughts you have—some might be just a word; others might be a sentence about the image or how the product fits within the image. Keep working this process, cut out more photos, and refine your search for types of images that might work. What would make someone believe your picture is true? How does it relate back to the consumer? Who would use the product in that situation? Do the images create any impulses within you?

Consider also the possibility of shooting your own library of images to help you in your thinking. When you go on vacation or on a business trip, take a camera with you and record images that make you think of emotional things. For example a church could mean to you sanctuary, beliefs, hope, love, etc...Another example might be a bridge: strength, willpower, technology, engineering, etc. You will find that as you shoot these images you will also be making decisions of how to shoot the product for the final idea. The angle, the color, the texture, or the background.

Exercise Two: Pictures & Music. Remember to begin with the Why, What, Where, When, and Who of the product!

Pictures, like music, can be a great place for emotional responses—thus a great place for ideas.

Let's begin by video recording some music videos from MTV, CMT and VH1. First watch the video from MTV. Write down any word, image, or emotion—anything that comes to mind. Now look at the video again, but this time with the volume turned down. What do the images say to you? How do they make you feel? How do the people within the images feel? Where are they going? Where have they been? What story are they telling? Ask all kinds of questions. You're looking for a place to begin, so the more you get involved in writing words relating to your impressions, the more places you'll have to start with.

Now rewind and just listen to the video. What is the music saying to you? How does it make you feel?

Now go back to your five W's and connect the dots. Is there anything there that could relate back to the product? Do any situations come to mind? Let loose, there is no right or wrong...just ideas for you to nurture later and make a great idea come to life. Say it out loud for all to hear or write it on a picture in big letters—what may seem silly or dumb to you may help someone else gel an idea together. Remember, we're looking for as many ideas as possible.

Now repeat the process with other videos.

Notes

6

The Product

✦

knowing the ins and outs
of your world

It's now time to look to the actual product/service for creative ideas. The product, after all, is our hero. The better you know the product, the better you can advertise it.

> *Real knowledge of a product, and of people in relation to it, is not easy to come by. Getting it is something like the process which was recommended to DeMaupassant as the way to learn to write. "Go out into the streets of Paris," he was told by an older writer, "and pick out a cab driver. He will look to you very much like every other cab driver. But study him until you can describe him so that he is seen in your description to be an individual, different from every other cab driver in the world."*
>
> *This is the real meaning of getting an intimate knowledge of a product and its consumer.*
>
> —James Web Young, A Technique for Producing Ideas[1]

Know the Client/Audience—Environment. Finding the buying button to sell to the audience/consumer is what makes up a great idea. A good way to understand why the customer might want your product or service is to experience the use or location. By going to a restaurant, a building/office, a warehouse/manufacturing facility and experiencing their environments, these areas will more than likely spawn some feeling in you. This is the same feeling that a consumer might have. This is important for you to know because understanding your consumer allows you to make a connection with them and by doing so, convince them to use your product or service. Keep it simple though. Knowing why someone would want the client's product will help you know how to sell, but first ask some questions of yourself. What's the client's impression of themselves? What is the product/service environment (where is it used)? What is your impression of the client? What is the consumer's impression (quality vs. cost, color/shape, convenience, features/benefits)? What is the environment (economy, competition, client's financial situation, supply vs. demand)? These are some of the questions to consider because the idea is in the answer. Because the answer is the idea, you have to spend most of your time NOT thinking of ideas but researching the client's product and getting to know their end user.

---

1.   A Technique for Producing Ideas by James Webb Young, page 33-34

If you know what your rival thinks he knows, and how strongly he believes in what he knows, you can reinforce or change those beliefs to your advantage.

—Descarte's formulation.[2]

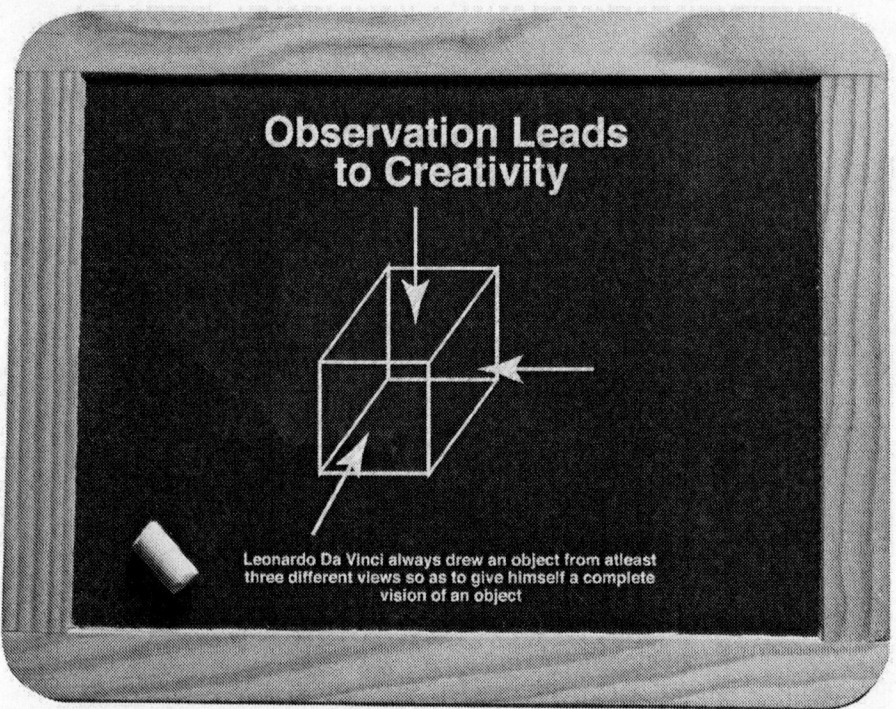

How do we look at a product from different angles? Glad you asked that question. First, test the product, Don't be shy, get in it, feel it, use it, taste it—get to know it. Write your impressions down, being as descriptive as possible. Ask yourself questions. Does the product line need to offer more colors or a better shape? What do you find appealing? What problems, if any, do you have with it? (If you're having problems with coming up with words, look to your why, what, when, where, and who's for help).

---

2.   The Octopus and the Orangutan, by Eugene Linden, page 141

Now, after you have exhausted all your descriptive capabilities, look at your list. Just by looking at the words you've jotted, can someone tell you what the product is? If not, you need to write some more.

Take some time and visit with the client and find out what their impression is of themselves. What is their corporate environment? Do all the employees wear suits to work or is it more casual attire around the office? How do people introduce themselves? Write all of this down and post it on the wall.

What is your client's financial situation? Are they doing a lot of new research, looking for new and better ideas or are they relying on just what they have to see them through?

Talk to your client's customers if possible and observe other people. What are other people saying about their product or service? Be the reporter on the street and investigate all avenues of the story. The truth is out there.

"Always ask better questions...you get better answers."[3]

Do their customers feel the product is costly or a good value for the money? A lot of the overall impressions of the consumer will rest in these questions being answered.

Does the product line need to offer more colors or a better shape? Color is a big influence on people's emotional state, so this may or may not be an issue. Better to find out all issues up front.

As in real estate, location can be a factor in sales. Take some time to see if location is affecting the sales of the product. Are people willing to drive to get the product or service? Are most sales done through the mail or the Internet? What does the client's location look like? If the client's business is new it will make a better impression than if it looks old or rundown. If the building is very artsy it will project a different impression than if it's a very open and spacious layout vs. a cramp looking office where everyone looks as if they are right on top of each other. Make a note of everything. We are looking for differences and facts about the environment in which the product or service lives. Location may be a big reason for sales.

---

3.   Tom Monaham "Creativety" Seminar 1997

In any environment, it's the survival of the fittest. What helps you to survive are the things that make you different or special from other things that do not do as well. Feature and or benefits—what makes us better than our competition? Why should we survive?

When talking about environment, we must consider the world's environment. What is happening in the world, in your country, your state, your city, and your neighborhood? The economic factors of the world will affect how we sell.

Know the competition. What are they doing to survive and win vs. us? This may be easy information to find or you may need to visit the competition and see what they are doing right and what they are doing wrong. You might find some insights that your client doesn't know about. Pass along any research revelations. Your client will be very grateful.

Consider supply and demand. One must be able to give the customer what they want. But, low supply can also be a good thing in that the price or service can fetch a higher price if and only if the consumer sees it as something that they cannot live without. Create a demand and you can create more profits and the need for more production.

A good investigative reporter like yourself should be able to find a great story to tell once you have all the facts to work with. Don't forget to write it all down for quick easy referral from time to time.

Now you have a master list of client impressions, product attributes and short-comings, plus descriptions, competitive impressions, etc. You have looked at the product from every angle possible—now you can advertise it with authority. You have lifted your limitations and are open to all possibilities.

Now, look to your master list. Circle any words that describe the product. Discard the shortcomings. We'll deal with these later. You are left with a list that should describe the product in a positive light. Go through each word or description and come up with as many other words or objects that describe it. Example: our product is a Sticky Bun. You taste it and jot down the words honey and sweet, along with a list of others. Looking at the word honey, you may write down bee, bee-hive, bear, or yummy. Now look to these words for ideas. Maybe the ad is of a Sticky Bun being swarmed by some bees. Or maybe it's of a bear that has discarded his honey pot for a Sticky Bun. Whatever the idea—write it down. Remember that we're looking for as many ideas that we can come up with.

Exercise One: Pick out any household object. Describe the object—writing down as many descriptive words you can in ten minutes. Now, give your list to a friend. Can they tell you what the object is?

Exercise Two: Pick a product. After completing exercise one. Circle the negatives and set aside. Now go through each descriptive word and come up with at least three words to describe them. From these words what ideas can you come up with?

Exercise Three (using the product and pictures): Complete exercise two, stopping before the idea stage. Go through books and magazines and cut out images that relate to the words you've come up with. Do these bring any ideas to mind? Can someone tell you what the product is from your pictures?

Notes

7

The Spokesperson

✦

the art of the celebrity & expert

One of the most powerful ways to persuade someone is to have a person say how well they enjoyed or appreciated something. It's part of human nature that wants to believe what we are told; because of this, testimonials have always been popular in selling a product. Leaders of countries and armies have long used the art of persuasion (Uncle Sam). Most people won't follow someone that they don't believe, at least a little. It is this fact that has drawn advertisers to use people of some power or prominence to sell their product (Donald Trump and McDonalds). Over the years, testimony from the famous, and infamous (remember Monica Lewinsky), in our society has expanded to include many other types of people including, but not limited to, actors, models, comedians, singers, sport stars, politicians, royalty, the dead, authors, teachers, business executives, and no names (people on the street). Celebrities tend to be the most popular because they have a built-in recognition, equity, if you will; and of course, everyone wants to be like Mike (Michael Jordon). Therefore, we use testimonials like public speakers to sell the features and benefits of a product vs. some other product out there.

If you/your client believe testimonials are the way to go, you need to anticipate that a good portion of your production budget will be used to pay the star. Stars cost money and often, lots of it. Remember, the spokesperson you choose for your product should be of good character (unless it is the infamy angle you desire). Many a product's allure has been lost due to controversy arising from a spokesperson's illegal activity or unacceptable morality. Make sure the entire person, including activities, is taken into account when picking the right person for your client's product.

Exercise One: Look to your product and develop your creative strategy (why, what, when, where, and who). Now describe your product in the manner that was used in Chapter six—the product. Remember to be specific and concise. Can a person look at your descriptions and tell you what the product is? The next step is to go through each descriptive word and attach a spokesperson(s) to each. Don't limit yourself to the obvious. Have some fun and just let the list, and your imagination, go wild. The more possibilities you have, the more likely you are to find the right person. And don't forget the dead. Did I say DEAD? Yes. With the power of today's technology, we can animate anyone and anything. An example of this is old movie footage of John Wayne mixed with a beer commercial, another is Fred Astir dancing with a vacuum cleaner. Plus, isn't impersonation the sincerest form of flattery?

You've made your list checked it twice now we're going to find out who's got what it takes. Choose the best one or two for now to work with. Write all the movies, championships, or awards they have won. Now let's think about what would they say about our product to convince us to by the product. Is it because we want to be like them? Is it that the celebrity spokesperson is an expert in their field? Is it that they make us feel good about ourselves? Can you trust them with your life, your kids, or your money? Finding why we would buy something from them is what makes them worth the money we have to pay them because Stars cost money.

Exercise Two: Check your list from exercise one against your creative strategy. Who stands out? Does anyone fit the product's image? Choose three people from your list to work with. Under each name, list anything you know about the person. What they have done. What they like. What they look like. The more the better. Now, let's think about what they would say about the product to convince someone to buy it. Go through each descriptive word(s) and match it up against the creative strategy. Do any words or situations come to mind? Remember, it's important to write it all down. We're looking for that place to begin.

Notes

8

Color

✦

using our beautiful world

He who loses his sight loses his view of the universe.

—Leonardo Da Vinci[1]

Color communicates and color sells—products, messages, ideas and environments. So, it should not be surprising that we should spend some time on color and its relationship to generating ideas. Colors by nature are evolutionary, changing gradually in step with environment, culture, social, economic and technological development. Color is a unique way to create an emotion by giving rise to desires that promote comfort, familiarity, home, security, heritage, optimism and, yes, innocence.

Color is part of many associations: women's fashion, interior/environmental furnishings and structures, products, and signs. Think of color as everything you view—every second of every day—which has an important message that your mind is using to evaluate and create impressions of the world around you. Now ask yourself if color can be an important selling tool to generate an idea.

People associate color like music with feelings. This allows us to use color in our ideas to stir emotions. Red = Anger/Love, Blue = Calmness/Violence, Yellow = Happiness/Sickness, and Green = Envy/Life. Every color can be seen as Black and as White. Good or Evil. When using color to generate ideas you must look at both sides.

Color, as you can see, relates to all things and because of this, we are able to use that in helping us to generate new thinking. It's this open thinking that will allow us to find the great idea to sell the product or service.

Exercise One: Pick a color to start with. How about red? Post a big spot on the wall and try to generate thoughts off of red by using the expanding universe as seen in chapter three. A helpful idea might also be to write all the thoughts inside that particular color. It can be things that are red or just things that make you see red. Examples can be a red rose = passion, love, lust, or want. Red balloon = freedom, expansion, joy, excitement, loss. Blood = death, kill, hurt, injury, anger, passion. Get the idea? Try to get at least 100 ideas from a color before moving on to another color. You will be tempted to say that I can't think of anything for

---

1.   How to think like Leonardo Da Vinci by Michael J. Gelb, Page 95

that color but take a minute to look at the world around you. Man has not created colors…he has only mimicked them. All colors originated in nature first.

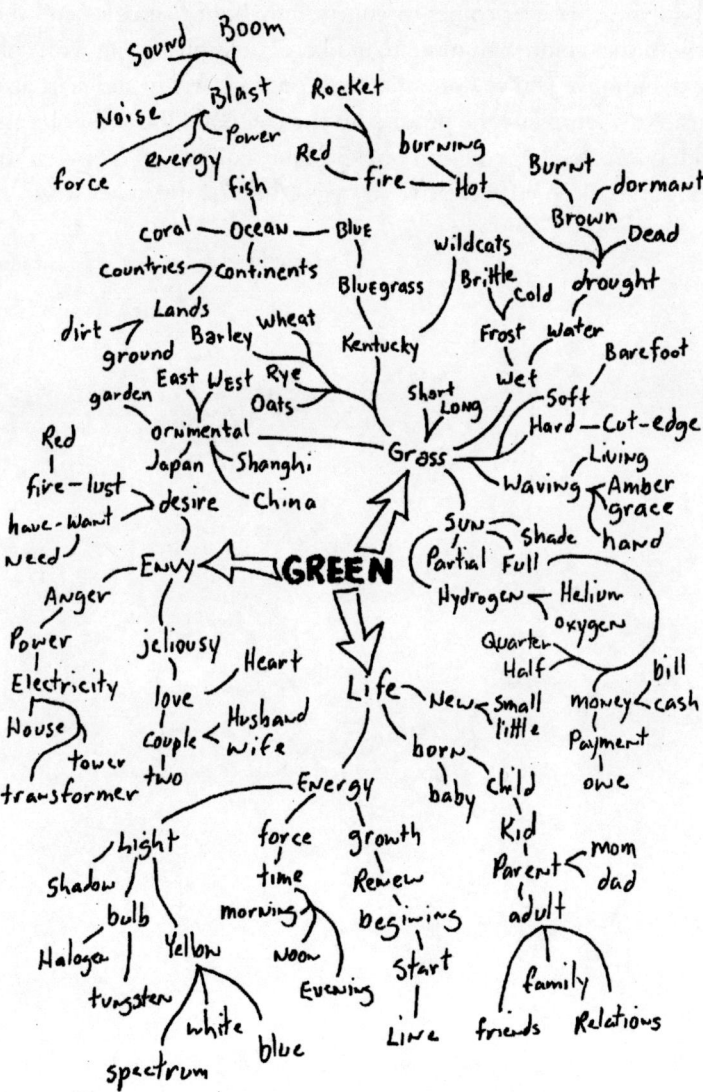

Exercise Two: Here's another way in which we can use color to generate new ideas. Use another color, for example: green. Grass might be the first thought in your mind. Now run with it before moving onto another green object: long/short, wet/frost, hard/soft, burnt/brown, cut/edge/waving/living/crab/Kentucky bluegrass/Rye Grass/Ornamental/Shade Grass/Full Sun/Partial Sun/etc. Make it about association with that color and don't try to edit anything at first—just write it all down, what ever comes to your mind about that color and the object associated with that color. You more than likely could fill a room with color association ideas and once you've done that pick the top twenty and start again with associations. Now lets relate the product to the color and the color objects you've been working on. See if you can make some correlation between the two. Remember—go back to your creative strategy (the Ws) if you get stuck.

Notes

9

Role Playing

◆

*thinking like the consumer
and your client!*

Role playing is about knowing everything about the product. To do this you have to think of yourself as the consumer of the product and what your wants and uses might be, then act out the uses. As well as, you have to look at where the client is coming from and why they think that their product fills a need in the market place. This can be a very fun way to open up and just let the ideas flow as you envision yourself as someone else. It's like being a kid again and pretending that you're not you.

This brainstorming technique works best in a group. Everyone should get involved and immersed in the strategy. Don't just think about ideas—work ideas through…how is the product used. Observe and make notes as to how everyone is using and experimenting with the product and who they are and why they are that person. You are looking for that insight into the consumer and the product that will make it stand out and be different.

Remember that a person who takes the time to look and get to know their universe can find that 'little something' that has great meaning.

…the curious end of restless man, Who for a second of galactic time

Floated upon a speck of cosmic dust Around a minor sun.

—Rosser Reeves[1]

Be willing to be curious and restless of the world.

Exercise One: Start the exercise by playing the consumer. Who are you? How do you dress? What is your education? Male/Female? Young/Old? Strong/Frail? Well spoken/Soft spoken? Talk through the consumer and how they are using the product. Use the product in your role-playing. If it's a cereal, get some milk, a bowl, a spoon and start eating. Test your competitor's brand in the same way. If you're a mother, how do you get your child to like a cereal that's good for them? If you're a kid how and why would you like or dislike the brand? What about packaging; colorful, fun, informative, has a prize inside?

---

1.   "The Poetry Side": Rosser Reeves to George Roche, October 23, 1962, Rosser Reeves Papers. The Mirror Makers by Stephen Fox, Page 191.

Exercise Two: Now try role playing as the client/salesperson selling the product. How would you sell it? Based on your sales pitch, what reasons would a customer give for not buying the product?

You can also role-play by using actual objects that the consumer would use. Make ties to the customer by holding things that they would have at their house. Not necessarily the product but, stuff they might have around our product or use in conjunction with our product. These things they use in their everyday lives, these associations will help to stimulate us into seeing how our customers lives are lived.

I listen from within.

—Thomas Alva Edison

Until we make a connection with our customer, we have no way in convincing them to do something we want them to do. If they have a lot of personal items we have to look at it differently than if they have just the necessities in life.

Exercise three: Walk through your own house to see what things you might use with the product. Place all the items you find on a table and spend some time looking at them. Just like we have before with pictures write down thoughts, words, or uses on a piece of paper and place it near each object. Once you've gone through all of the objects and have placed a card next to it, see if you can connect the dots with the five W's and the words and statements you wrote for them.

If you have no objects that your consumer would use around your own house (I would find that hard to believe since all of us share many things in life), go to the store where they would shop. What would they buy for themselves?

Notes

10

Personal Experiences and the Familiar

✦

using what you know

Most of us have had some, often first hand, experience with most product categories. You can use these personal experiences to relate to the product and develop ideas. Example: if the product you're currently working on is for a soap manufacturer, you can use your personal experience using soap, smelling soap, etc. to springboard off. Look into your past and find things about the soaps you have used. Think of your five senses—sight, sound, taste, touch and smell—was there a time when these senses might have come in contact with the product?

We keep moving forward, opening new doors and doing new things, because we're curious.

—Walt Disney[1]

Use your own personal experiences as testimonials for the consumer. Remember—people want to know the experiences of other people and what that outcome has produced. Was there a time in your life when you did not have the product, but if you did, your situation would have been better? Let's look again at soap.

Some time ago, while putting a new roof on my house, I found as I broke for lunch that my hands had not only dirt from handling the old shingles but tar from the new shingles I had spent all morning laying. While trying to clean my hands, I found that the dirt came off easily but that the tar was much tougher to get rid of. After finding out that three different soaps had no effect, or little, I tried Brand X. Brand X with special porous materials and a special ingredient removed the tar with ease. While working on ideas for the soap client, I was able to use my own experience with soap as a starting point for ideas.

George Johnson noted, "explaining the strange in terms of the familiar—that is the essence of the quest…using metaphor and analogy, the tools of artists.[2]

Our own experiences can help us create an idea. What is familiar to us can also be familiar to the customer as well. Stories, especially ones with a semblance of truth, help put people into the same situation that you were in. It gives them a point of reference that can be used to relate back to their own personal experiences. By finding in ourselves times that the product made life better for us, the

---

1.   Thinking out of the box by Mike Vance and Diane Deacon, page 19
2.   The Octopus and the Orangutan, by Eugene Linden, page 15

consumer can see how the product might make sense for them in the same or similar situations.

Exercise: Begin with a period in your life that you have a lot of memories of—we'll use High School. Whether good or bad we all have a memory of High School, and it's a period in life that most everyone can relate to. A lot of things changed in those years—our hairstyles, our dress code, friendships, our relationships (first love/crushes). Now, let's use these memories to make a connection with the product we are trying to sell. If you look at the product closely and think back to High School, did you use the product back then? Why or why not? Was it something you relied on? Who was using it back then? Was it even available? Use your life experiences from that time period and try to write a story, at least a few lines, about it. Like always, just write it down—don't edit yourself as to whether it works or not. We'll come back to it later after we create a couple more stories, then we'll make them more current and relevant to today's situation.

To the right is an example of an ad in which using one's life experiences with a little manipulation can give an ad a more personal feel.

Headline: My First Love.
Body Copy: I was 16. I remember sitting in traffic, four lanes deep on each side, just looking to meet girls and show off the new car. I used to get out, talk to girls and come back a half-hour later, only to find nothing had moved.

For over 60 years, auto insurance from AAA of Michigan has kept the romance going on Michigan's roads.

So Betty Sue said yes, she'd go to the drive-in with me. The whole gang was there. The movie's over and I wanted to be cool, so I floored it. Tore outta there with the speaker still hooked to the window, its cable flopping in the wind.

And to keep the relationship fresh, AAA Michigan auto insurance has a tradition of quality customer service, including fast, courteous claims processing.

Now we're sitting in the diner, and outside there's a squeal of brakes and a crash. Six guys run outside with the same thought—"Please, God, not mine." But, it was mine, and I remember saying, "She'll never be right again."

In addition, the AAA Auto Club offers variable extras like Triptiks, Tour Books, Traveler Cheques, and special AAA Michigan member discounts; just show us your card.

Last week, I came home to find a dent on the fender and a note on the windshield. In my wife's handwriting, it said, "Sorry."…I brought it back from the shop this afternoon. Darned if AAA didn't handle the claim as fast today as they did then.

And a funny thought occurred to me. I've driven five cars in my lifetime. But, you know, you never forget your first.

If you would like to keep the romance going, find out more about auto insurance from AAA Michigan.

Notes

11

Opposite Thinking

✦

the positive side of negative

Opposites attract. Just when you think you've exhausted all the possibilities, try opposite thinking. If you've decided white is the right background color, make it black and see what you can do with it. If you're showing a photo of a person on a sunny beach, what if you put them in the middle of the arctic with only the northern lights? This is opposite thinking.

Creative Geniuses Think In Opposites. According to David Bohm, geniuses are able to think differently because they can tolerate ambivalence between two incompatible subjects.[1]

Opposite Thiking can be a lot of fun because it allows you to take the negative side, and sometimes the positive approach, to ask all the hard questions. Often, you are asking the questions that clients will ask about your ideas. Why won't they work? What's wrong with this picture? Our image is of a higher standard than what you are showing. Why have you chosen that color for the background or for our product? Play devil's advocate before you get with a client and your ideas may not die an early death. Many times in the opposite you will find a better idea than the original, by thinking and asking what's right or wrong with this?

Incompatibles often can be made compatible. Opposites can attract because two sides are better than one. Think of this not as a compromise of the idea but as the marriage of two lovers.

Black & White—Half of each idea shows up in the final idea. An example of this is when the story does a twist. Many times in movies we are swept away with who is the bad guy only to learn later that the bad guy is, in reality, the hero. The victim becomes the aggressor in the end. The tortoise beats the faster hare in a race. So on and so forth…you get the point. Backgrounds and other images work in much the same way. Half the ad could be the positives about the product and the other half could be the negative about the competition. Or maybe it's just a sunny day with the product being used vs. a rainy day and the product's performance in those conditions.

Whatever way you start your thinking, with either positive or negative, after awhile try Opposite Thinking.

---

1.   Recognizing Creative Genius by Paul Matthaeus, Communication Arts January/February 1999 page 49

Exercise One: Take the existing advertising campaign for the product you have to advertise and look at it in an opposite direction. Whatever you find positive about the ad, write it down—then turn that into a list of as many negatives as you can. List them next to each positive. As you create this list of negatives, see how you can improve on the positives. What if you: change the color of the field (background), change the location of where the photograph was taken (warm client vs. cold, mountains vs. ocean, or forest vs. desert), move the logo and change it's size, and change the gender of talent or even just their ages? What about the headline—did it capture you? Break the headline down—what words were good, what turned you off?

You are now looking at the ad like the consumer will. They immediately decide what they like and dislike, from there they decide whether or not to read or listen further to your message. By knowing where you are coming from you can have somewhere to go.

Exercise Two: If the product is completely new and no work exists on it, you can still invert your thinking 180°. We do this by using just the product itself. Make a list of everything you see about the product. What's the name of it? What color is it? What are the features of the label? What does it do? Does it have any competition (if yes, get their ads and do exercise one as well)? What are the product features? What makes it new and different?

Next do the negative exercise and list all the opposites. When you were thinking of negatives did some positive ideas come to mind? Put them on another list for how you are going to sell this idea to a consumer. Opposite Thinking is about changing perceptions, yours and theirs.

Notes

12

Hard Sell

✦

more than just screaming

Okay, let's go for the jugular. Hit them with the sledgehammer. What are the facts? Let's make the client's product the true hero. Use the following format to achieve the hard sell—show the product, show the product, and show the product. Let's figure out how to show the product in the best light possible if the product is all we are going to show. Look at this objectively, can we use its shape, its color, its size vs. other objects or competitors, or does it have a unique texture that makes it different from all others of its kind?

In the hard sell, the product's shape can be an enticing feature. For instance, many times in automotive advertising you will see very sexy close-up shots of the sheet metal, headlights, instrument panels, or leather seats. These close-ups are used because people love their cars and if an advertiser shows you how good their car looks, it might get you to consider theirs. Another example would be the close-ups you see for food advertising. My, those burgers look good. To use shape as an idea starter get a digital camera and shoot all kinds of tight shots and pin them up to the board. When you stand back take some time to stare at them…they will more than likely bring ideas of other objects that they look like. Remember all the times when you sat and stared at the clouds and made animals and ships or landscape scenes. Shape is a hard sell in that the product is the hero all the way through, but done right, shape can be a very interesting idea if we find the feature that tells the best story.

Just like shape, the color or colors of the product can be used in interesting ways. Imagine using all the colors in a Kaleidoscope and having them mix in different ways throughout the ad. They could be blurred or just a collage of images strung together in an interesting pattern. Just like with shape, take some full image shots of the product and cut them apart with a pair of scissors, then rearrange the pieces to see if an interesting idea arises.

Size and the use of angles to create a distorted image of the product can change our idea of what we think about something. If research shows that people think our product looks small, shoot it tight to make it look big. If it's not tough enough, shoot it from a very low angle and it will look big and tough. Zooming in and out while at the same time panning around the product fast and at varying speeds can do size and shape used together in unison.

Hard sell can also be yelling and selling, whether you like it or not this can be very effective in meeting the requirements of the strategy questions.

"Make the most of yourself, for that is all there is of you."

—Ralph Waldo Emerson

Exercise One: Take a product and use it's shape, color and texture to tell a story. What can you do to get the product's image across through the use of shape, color, or texture?

Notes

13

Idea Refinement

✦

making it all work

"I don't want people who do the right things. I want people who do inspiring things…let us blaze new trails."

—Bill Bernbach[1]

Once we have an idea how can we refine it? One very good way is to get other people's opinions. Use their experiences and knowledge to improve the idea. Expanding the idea through the use of a group allows you to use their knowledge in conjunction with yours, making the universe that much bigger. We can also use other idea development techniques to refine our idea. Ask the hard questions: does it help the customer? Does it work for the client's needs? Is it on strategy? Always remember, we begin with strategy (the five W's) and we end with it. Once you have the ideas, do they fit the strategy that you started with? Do you need to go back to the strategy and refine it some more as well as refine the idea?

The refinement stage is when we look to make it not only new or unique but also interesting. What do I mean by interesting? No matter how good an idea is, if it is not interesting or attention getting it does not work. If no one pays attention to your message, you haven't done your job as a communicator and story-teller. Make it funny; make it emotional (use little kids or animals); sex sells (or so they say); make it hip/trendy. The list can go on forever. The key is to make people want to look at and listen to your idea. They'll only buy it if they buy into your idea!

We've all consumers. And we respond instinctively. We like an idea that touches us, amuses us, surprises us, impresses us.

—Diane Rothchild[2]

Refine, refine, and refine. Re-write. Re-look at it. Re-think it. Don't settle for your first idea or your second or even your third. Work on it till it's great. Generate a thousand ideas. Then narrow them to one hundred ideas and I guarantee at least a couple of them will be worthwhile. And ONE will be great. A real winner and the big idea that will change a business.

---

1.   "The Mirror Makers" By Stephen Fox. Published by William Morrow and Company, Inc. Page 241
2.   Diane Rothchild—Quotation

Show me a thoroughly satisfied man and I will show you a failure.

—Thomas Alva Edison

Exercise One: Take one of the products and the ideas you generated for it from a previous exercise. Choose ten of the ideas and match against the creative strategy you devised for that product. One by one, take each idea and ask yourself if it answers the issues brought up in the 'why' portion of the strategy. Example: our product is Goodness Gracious Cream Bar. Our 'why' strategy may include: to enhance the low fat benefits of the candy; tie-in with the organic ingredients of the bar; and build upon the energy enhancing benefits of the candy. We would look at each of our ideas and see if they build upon each portion of the strategy. If the idea doesn't answer a part of the strategy, is there a way to make it work? Maybe through a copy revision, a visual change, or even the use of multiple spots or ads. Maybe it doesn't work. If not set it aside and move on.

Notes

14

Conclusion

Now that we have our idea, let's move forward with it! Time to produce a commercial, a print ad, a web page, or a new product? Not quite!

There's a time to test an idea's validity, and it's not during the early stages of the creative process. All ideas have flaws in the beginning if we look for them. The challenge is to not look for flaws in your ideas until they have had time to grow. Even when an idea is not perfect at the moment of conception with a little more constructive brainstorming that idea can take the high pedestal of greatness. Try to be conscious of prejudging an idea and hold off evaluation as long as you can. You will be surprised at how many ideas look better in the light of the next day.

We all get attached to how things are meant to be done. We do not always look for a new way of doing things. When people resist change, they inevitably hold back improvement.

The Final Stage. The last stage through which you pass to complete the idea-producing process: the stage which might be called the cold, gray dawn of the morning after.

In this stage you take your little newborn idea out into the world of reality. And when you do you usually find that it is not quite the marvelous child it seemed when you first gave birth to it.

> It requires a deal of patient working to make most ideas fit the exact conditions, or the practical exigencies, under which they must work. And here is where many good ideas are lost.
>
> —James Webb Young[1]

Often, the "craziest" ideas are closer to "genius" than the same old "this is the way it's done" ideas. Sometimes brainstorming generates ideas that "don't make sense" and quite often seem "silly" or "wrong", but give these seeds the chance to grow. You might find a 'mighty Oak' that can stand the tests of time is inside one of them. Good luck and let's look for the big idea that will change a client's business and maybe change a generation (or at least sell some toilet paper).

---

1.   A Technique for Producing Ideas by James Webb Young, page 52

We do not know one millionth of one percent about anything.

—Thomas Alva Edison

Dare Mighty Things.

Notes

Bibliography

A Technique for Producing Ideas, By James Webb Young. Special 1994 Edition. Published by NTC business books. Pages 25, 30, 33-34, 48, 52.

How Do You Get Ideas? Zen and the art of advertising, By Robyn Griggs in the publication "AGENCY" Fall 1996, Page 36

Murry Gelberg, Graphic Design, May 2002, Page 35
Murry Gelberg, Ignition a publication from SAPPI Paper

Quote by: Jim Bosha, Executive VP Executive Creative Director, Campbell Mithun Esty, Minneapolis

Recognizing Creative Genius, By Paul Matthaeus. Communication Arts January/February 1999, Page 49

Diane Rothchild—Quotation 1994 at a conference
The Mirror Makers, By Stephen Fox. Published by William Morrow and Company, Inc. Page 241

How to Think like Leonardo DiVinci, By Michael J. Gelb. Published by Dell Publishing a division of Random House, Inc. Page 95

How to think out of the Box, By Mike Vance and Diane Deacon, Published by Career Press. Page 190

Quote by: Andrew Jaffe, Executive Director, Clio Awards, Publishing Director of Adweek Books—2002

Ogilvy on Advertising, By David Ogilvy

Priceless: Turning Ordinary Products into Extraordinary Experiences, By Diana Lasalle and Terry A. Britton

A Whack on the Side of the Head & a Kick in the Seat of the Pants, By Roger Von Oech

The Art of Creative Thinking, By Wilfred Peterson

The Magic of Thinking Big, By David Schwartz
Graphic Design:usa, Published by Kaye Publishing Corporation
Communication Arts Magazine, Published by Coyne & Blanchard, Inc.

Adweek, Published by VNU business publications

PRINT, Published by RC Publications, Inc.

The Octopus and the Orangutan—More true tales of animal intrigue, intelligence, and ingenuity, By Eugene Linden, Pages 15 & 141

I would like to credit a number of people in this book for I am an accumulation of everything I have ever heard, seen and experienced. And I would like to give them all credit because, without their teachings I wouldn't be who I am today.

—TIM

Manley Mitton. Creative Mentor. Thank you Manley, for stopping in once a week after your retirement to work with me on my art direction and graphic design skills. Your fifty years of experience put me five years ahead of my peers with the knowledge you worked on passing on to me.

Jack DiGeussepe. Executive Creative Director, friend, and mentor. His wealth of knowledge and many stories helped to shape my way of thinking about generating great creative for clients as well as boosting clients' profits. Plus, showing me how to have some fun in doing it!

Garry Nelson. Creative Director. Your knowledge on client presentations and how to listen to what clients want has been invaluable to me in my many years in client meetings and presentations.

George Piliouras. Sr. Partner/Executive Creative Director. Your energy at client presentations and your drive for that idea that will change the client business will always be memorable to me.

Antoni Louw. Louw's Management Corporation. Vail, Arizona 85641 "How to Sell Great Creative". I wish to give Antoni credit not from anything specifically written but, through a workshop I have had with him he has added to my wealth of knowledge.
www.louwsmanagement.com

Tom Monaham. "Creativity" Seminar speaker on creative techniques. And as with everything—we all combine what works for us from various sources to make it into a new process of doing something. I am a piece of you and the many years of hard work you put into your creative thought starters.

To all the creative people I have had the honor and pleasures to work with over my many years in this business you are all Mighty Thinkers. Keep up the good work!

Related Reading:

Unfortunately, at the time of publishing, we have not been able to read all of the books listed below but, they are recommended reading by colleagues and associates.

Aha! 10 Ways to Free Your Spirit & Find Your Great Ideas,
By Jordan Ayan

The Creative Mind—Myths and Mechanisms,
By Margaret Boden

The Do-It-Yourself Labotomy,
By Tom Monahan

Jump Start Your Brain,
By Doug Hall with David Wecker

The Creative Brain,
By Ned Herman

Wake Up Your Creative Genius,
By Kurt Hanks and Jay Parry

Why Didn't I Think of That?,
By Charles McCoy

The Art and Science of Creativity,
By George Kneller

Lateral Thinking—Creativity Step by Step,
By Edward De Bono

The Creative Problem Solver's Toolbox,
By Richard Fobes

About the Authors

Timothy Cory has twenty-five-plus years in the advertising profession as Associate Creative Director, Senior Art Director, and Executive Producer. Currently, Tim has a senior position on the Ford business at J. Walter Thompson in Detroit. His experience is wide-ranging, including work with many Fortune 500 clients like IBM, Coca-Cola, ITT Automotive, as well as Big Boy Restaurants, Detroit Diesel Allison, ECCS Computers, and Citrus Strip products.

Having been honored with many awards, Tim's winning ideas have helped clients sell more and grow their business. His work, both in print and broadcast mediums, has been featured prominently in numerous national trade magazines.

Thomas Slater has over twenty years broadcast experience, including fifteen years in advertising as a Senior Writer and Creative Supervisor at J. Walter Thompson in Detroit. Primarily an automotive ad expert, Tom's other accounts have included Precision Tune, Pet Supplies Plus and RE/MAX. A talk-show producer before his life in advertising, he escaped just before the current glut of mediocrity.

The authors have put these techniques to work as a team at J. Walter Thompson. Together they also teach these techniques in a course titled Brainstorming at the Agency at the College for Creative Studies in the Cultural Center of Downtown Detroit. Working to help the next generation of AD People set the bar higher.

We encourage you to make notes in this book and refer back to them often. Diagram your own ideas and processes and save them for future Brainstorming sessions.

We all think in different ways and it is that fact that allows for unlimited possibilities and creativity.

Notes

Notes

Notes

Notes

Notes

Notes

Notes

Notes

Notes

Notes

Notes

0-595-29831-1

Printed in the United Kingdom
by Lightning Source UK Ltd.
103656UKS00001B/194